The approved documents

WITHDRAWN

What is an approved document?

The Secretary of State has approved a series of documents that give practical guidance about how to meet the requirements of the Building Regulations 2010 for England. Approved documents give guidance on each of the technical parts of the regulations and on regulation 7 (see the back of this document).

Approved documents set out what, in ordinary circumstances, may be accepted as reasonable provision for compliance with the relevant requirements of the Building Regulations to which they refer. If you follow the guidance in an approved document, there will be a presumption of compliance with the requirements covered by the guidance. However, compliance is not guaranteed; for example, 'normal' guidance may not apply if the particular case is unusual in some way.

Note that there may be other ways to comply with the requirements – *there is no obligation to adopt any particular solution contained in an approved document.* If you prefer to meet a relevant requirement in some other way than described in an approved document, you should discuss this with the relevant building control body.

In addition to guidance, some approved documents include provisions that must be followed exactly, as required by regulations or where methods of test or calculation have been prescribed by the Secretary of State.

Each approved document relates only to the particular requirements of the Building Regulations that the document addresses. However, building work must also comply with any other applicable requirements of the Building Regulations.

How to use this approved document

This document uses the following conventions.

a. Text against a green background is an extract from the Building Regulations 2010 or the Building (Approved Inspectors etc.) Regulations 2010 (both as amended). These extracts set out the legal requirements of the regulations.

b. Key terms, printed in green, are defined in Appendix A.

c. When this approved document refers to a named standard or other document, the relevant version is listed in Appendix E (documents referred to) and Appendix F (standards referred to) respectively. However, if the issuing body has revised or updated the listed version of the standard, you may use the new version as guidance if it continues to address the relevant requirements of the Building Regulations.

d. Additional *commentary in italic text* appears after some numbered paragraphs. This commentary is intended to assist understanding of the immediately preceding paragraph or sub-paragraph, or to direct readers to sources of additional information, but is not part of the technical guidance itself.

NOTE: *Standards and technical approvals may also address aspects of performance or matters that are not covered by the Building Regulations, or they may recommend higher standards than required by*

Where you can get further help

If you do not understand the technical guidance or other information in this approved document or the additional detailed technical references to which it directs you, you can seek further help through a number of routes, some of which are listed below:

a. The Planning Portal website: www.planningportal.gov.uk.

b. *If you are the person undertaking the building work:* either from your local authority building control service or from an approved inspector.

c. *If you are registered with a competent person scheme:* from the scheme operator.

d. *If your query is highly technical:* from a specialist or an industry technical body for the relevant subject.

The Building Regulations

The following is a high level summary of the Building Regulations relevant to most types of building work. Where there is any doubt you should consult the full text of the regulations, available at www.legislation.gov.uk.

Building work

Regulation 3 of the Building Regulations defines 'building work'. Building work includes:

a. the erection or extension of a building

b. the provision or extension of a controlled service or fitting

c. the material alteration of a building or a controlled service or fitting.

Regulation 4 states that building work should be carried out in such a way that, when work is complete:

a. for new buildings or work on a building that complied with the applicable requirements of the Building Regulations: the building complies with the applicable requirements of the Building Regulations.

b. for work on an existing building that did not comply with the applicable requirements of the Building Regulations:

(i) the work itself must comply with the applicable requirements of the Building Regulations

(ii) the building must be no more unsatisfactory in relation to the requirements than before the work was carried out.

Material change of use

Regulation 5 defines a 'material change of use' in which a building or part of a building that was previously used for one purpose will be used for another.

The Building Regulations set out requirements that must be met before a building can be used for a new purpose. To meet the requirements, the building may need to be upgraded in some way.

Materials and workmanship

In accordance with regulation 7, building work must be carried out in a workmanlike manner using adequate and proper materials. Guidance on materials and workmanship is given in Approved Document 7.

Energy efficiency requirements

Part 6 of the Building Regulations imposes additional specific requirements for energy efficiency.

If a building is extended or renovated, the energy efficiency of the existing building or part of it may need to be upgraded.

Notification of work

Most building work and material changes of use must be notified to a building control body unless one of the following applies.

a. It is work that will be self-certified by a registered competent person or certified by a registered third party.

b. It is work exempted from the need to notify by regulation 12(6A) of, or schedule 4 to, the Building Regulations.

Responsibility for compliance

People who are responsible for building work (for example the agent, designer, builder or installer) must ensure that the work complies with all applicable requirements of the Building Regulations. The building owner may also be responsible for ensuring that work complies with the Building Regulations. If building work does not comply with the Building Regulations, the building owner may be served with an enforcement notice.

Contents

Approved Document L2A: Conservation of fuel and power in new buildings other than dwellings

Summary

0.1 This approved document is one of four approved documents that give guidance on how to comply with the energy efficiency requirements of the Building Regulations:

Approved Document L1A: Conservation of fuel and power in new dwellings

Approved Document L1B: Conservation of fuel and power in existing dwellings

Approved Document L2A: Conservation of fuel and power in new buildings other than dwellings

Approved Document L2B: Conservation of fuel and power in existing buildings other than dwellings

The approved documents are supported by the:

Domestic Building Services Compliance Guide

Non-Domestic Building Services Compliance Guide

0.2 This approved document contains the following sections:

Section 1 sets out the relevant legal requirements and provides an overview of the steps to demonstrate compliance.

Section 2 sets out the considerations that apply to demonstrating that the design of the building will meet the energy efficiency requirements.

Section 3 sets out the considerations that apply when demonstrating that the design has been appropriately translated into actual construction performance.

Section 4 describes the information that should be provided to occupiers to help them achieve reasonable standards of energy efficiency in practice.

Section 5 provides a pointer to some useful information on different design approaches to meeting the energy efficiency requirements.

Appendix A: Key terms and abbreviations

Appendix B: Guidance on the types of building work covered by this approved document

Appendix C: Guidance on the types of buildings that are exempt from the energy efficiency requirements

Appendix D: Reporting evidence of compliance

Appendix E: Documents referred to

Appendix F: Standards referred to

Energy performance certificates

0.3 Regulation 29 of the Building Regulations requires that, subject to the exemptions set out at Appendix C, when a building is erected the person carrying out the work must give an energy performance certificate to the owner of the building and a notice to the building control body (BCB) that a certificate has been given including the reference number under which the certificate has been registered. See also the Energy Performance of Buildings (England and Wales) Regulations 2012 (SI 2012/3118) at www.legislation.gov.uk and detailed guidance on energy performance certificates at www.planningportal.gov.uk

Section 1: The requirements

1.1 This approved document, which takes effect on 6 April 2014, deals with the energy efficiency requirements in the Building Regulations 2010. Regulation 2(1) of the Building Regulations defines the energy efficiency requirements as the requirements of regulations 23, 25A, 25B, 26, 26A, 28, 29 and 40 and Part L of Schedule 1. The energy efficiency requirements relevant to the guidance in this approved document, which deals with new buildings, are those in regulations 25A, 26, 29 and 40 and Part L of Schedule 1, and are set out below.

NOTE: *Regulation 25B 'Nearly zero-energy requirements for new buildings' will not come into force until 2019 at the earliest. Statutory guidance on compliance with regulation 25B is not included within this approved document and will be provided nearer to the time that regulation 25B comes into force.*

1.2 Relevant extracts from the Building Regulations 2010 or the Building (Approved Inspectors etc.) Regulations 2010 (both as amended) are set out using text against a green background in this approved document. Where there is any doubt you should consult the full text of the regulations, available at www.legislation.gov.uk

Part L of Schedule 1: Conservation of fuel and power

Requirement	Limits on application
Schedule 1 – Part L Conservation of fuel and power	
L1. Reasonable provision shall be made for the conservation of fuel and power in buildings by:	
(a) limiting heat gains and losses–	
(i) through thermal elements and other parts of the building fabric; and	
(ii) from pipes, ducts and vessels used for space heating, space cooling and hot water services;	
(b) providing fixed building services which–	
(i) are energy efficient,	
(ii) have effective controls; and	
(iii) are commissioned by testing and adjusting as necessary to ensure they use no more fuel and power than is reasonable in the circumstances.	

Demonstrating compliance

1.3 In the Secretary of State's view, compliance with the energy efficiency requirements could be demonstrated by meeting the five separate criteria set out in the following paragraphs. Compliance software should produce an output report to assist BCBs check that compliance has been achieved.

NOTE: *The output report can benefit both developers and BCBs during the design and construction stages as well as at completion.*

1.4 Criterion 1: in accordance with regulation 26, the calculated CO_2 emission rate for the building (the Building CO_2 Emission Rate, BER) must not be greater than the Target CO_2 Emission Rate (TER), which is determined by following the procedures set out in paragraphs 2.7 to 2.36.

NOTE: *Criterion 1 is a regulation and is therefore mandatory, whereas the limits on design flexibility for Criteria 2 are statutory guidance. The calculations required as part of the procedure used to show compliance with this criterion can also provide information needed to prepare the* energy performance certificate *required by regulation 29 of the Building Regulations and by the Energy Performance of Buildings (England and Wales) Regulations 2012 (SI 2012/3118).*

1.5 Criterion 2: the performance of the individual fabric elements and the fixed building services of the building should achieve reasonable overall standards of energy efficiency, following the procedure set out in paragraphs 2.37 to 2.49.

NOTE: *Criterion 2 is intended to place limits on design flexibility to discourage excessive and inappropriate trade-offs. For example, individual building fabric elements with poor insulation standards being offset by renewable energy systems with uncertain service lives. This emphasises the purpose of Criterion 2.*

1.6 Criterion 3: demonstrate that the building has appropriate passive control measures to limit solar gains. The guidance given in paragraphs 2.50 to 2.53 of this approved document provides a way of demonstrating that suitable provisions have been made.

NOTE: *The purpose is to limit solar gains to reasonable levels during the summer period, in order to reduce the need for, or the installed capacity of, air-conditioning systems.*

1.7 Criterion 4: the performance of the building, as built, should be consistent with the BER. The guidance in Section 3 can be used to show that this criterion has been met. Extra credits will be given in the TER/BER calculation where builders can provide robust evidence of quality-assured procedures in the design and construction phases.

1.8 Criterion 5: the necessary provisions for enabling energy-efficient operation of the building should be put in place. The procedures described in Section 4 can be used to show that this criterion has been met.

Section 2: Design standards

Regulations 24 and 25

2.1 Regulations 24 and 25 state that:

> **Methodology of calculation of the energy performance of buildings**
>
> **24.** (1) The Secretary of State shall approve—
>
> (a) a methodology of calculation of the energy performance of buildings, including methods for calculating asset ratings and operational ratings of buildings; and
>
> (b) ways in which the energy performance of buildings, as calculated in accordance with the methodology, shall be expressed.
>
> (2) In this regulation—
>
> 'asset rating' means a numerical indicator of the amount of energy estimated to meet the different needs associated with a standardised use of the building; and
>
> 'operational rating' means a numerical indicator of the amount of energy consumed during the occupation of the building over a period of time.

> **Minimum energy performance requirements for buildings**
>
> **25.** Minimum energy performance requirements shall be set by the Secretary of State, in accordance with the methodology approved pursuant to regulation 24, for—
>
> (a) new buildings (which shall include new dwellings), in the form of target CO_2 emission rates; and
>
> (b) new dwellings, in the form of target fabric efficiency rates.

Target CO_2 Emission Rate (TER)

2.2 The Target CO_2 Emission Rate (TER) is the minimum energy performance requirement for a new building based on the methodology approved by the Secretary of State in accordance with regulation 25. It is expressed in terms of the mass of CO_2 emitted per year per square metre of the total useful floor area of the building.

2.3 The TER must be calculated using one of the calculation tools included in the methodology approved by the Secretary of State for calculating the energy performance of buildings pursuant to regulation 24. Those tools include:

a. the *Simplified Building Energy Model* (SBEM) for those buildings whose design features are capable of being adequately modelled by SBEM; or

b. other software tools approved under the *Notice of Approval*.

2.4 From time to time further software may be approved. An up-to-date list can be found on the Department for Communities and Local Government webpages at www.gov.uk

2.5 As part of the submission to a BCB, the applicant must show that the software tool used is appropriate to the application.

2.6 The TER is established by using approved software to calculate the CO_2 emission rate from a notional building of the same size and shape as the actual building, but with specified properties. These specified properties shall be as set out in the *National Calculation Methodology (NCM) modelling guide*, in the section headed 'Detailed definition of Notional Building for buildings other than dwellings'. The key components of the notional building specification can also be seen at Table 5. The TER is set equal to the CO_2 emissions from this notional building, with no further adjustment being made.

NOTE: *The TER is based on a building of the same size and shape as the actual building, constructed to a concurrent specification. This concurrent specification for Part L 2013 is given in the NCM modelling guide. Developers are still given the freedom to vary the specification, provided the same overall level of CO_2 emissions is achieved or bettered.*

Criterion 1 – Achieving the TER

2.7 Regulation 26 states that:

> **CO_2 emission rates for new buildings**
>
> **26.** Where a building is erected, it shall not exceed the target CO_2 emission rate for the building that has been approved pursuant to regulation 25.

Calculating the CO_2 emissions from the actual building

2.8 To demonstrate that the requirement in regulation 26 has been met, the actual Building CO_2 Emission Rate (BER) must be no greater (no worse) than the TER calculated as set out in paragraphs 2.2 to 2.6.

2.9 The BER must be calculated using the same calculation tool as used for establishing the TER.

2.10 In order to determine the BER, the CO_2 emission factors shall be as specified in Table 12 in *The Government's Standard Assessment Procedure for energy rating of dwellings*, SAP 2012.

2.11 When systems are capable of being fired by more than one fuel, then:

a. Where a biomass heating appliance is supplemented by an alternative appliance (e.g. gas), the CO_2 emission factor for the overall heating system should be based on a weighted average for the two fuels based on the anticipated usage of those fuels. The BER submission should be accompanied by a report, signed by a suitably qualified person, detailing how the combined emission factor has been derived.

b. Where the same appliance is capable of burning both biomass fuel and fossil fuel, the CO_2 emission factor for dual-fuel appliances should be used, except where the building is in a smoke control area, when the anthracite figure should be used.

c. In all other cases, the fuel with the highest CO_2 emission factor should be used.

NOTE: *This option is to cover dual-fuel systems where the choice of fuel actually used depends on prevailing market prices.*

2.12 If thermal energy is supplied from a district or community heating or cooling system, emission factors should be determined by considering the particular details of the scheme. Calculations should take account of the annual average performance of the whole system (i.e. the distribution circuits and all the heat generating plant, including any Combined Heat and Power (CHP), and any waste heat recovery or heat dumping). The predicted effect of all buildings proposed to be newly connected to the system in the first 12 months of operation of the system can be considered in the calculation of the percentage of heat supplied so that the increased operation of any marginal plant (e.g. gas boilers) is properly accounted for. The electricity generated by any CHP or trigeneration scheme is always credited at an emission factor equal to the grid average. CO_2 emissions associated with the thermal energy streams of a trigeneration scheme should be attributed in proportion to the output energy streams. The BER submission should be accompanied by a report, signed by a suitably qualified person, detailing how the emission factors have been derived.

NOTE: *This means that if a scheme burns F kWh of input fuel to produce E kWh of electricity and H kWh of useful heat (excluding heat rejected), the emission factor for the heat output should be taken as $1/H \times (F \times CO_{2F} - E \times CO_{2E})$ where CO_{2F} is the emission factor for the input fuel, and CO_{2E} the factor for grid electricity. See the NCM modelling guide at www.ncm.bre.co.uk.*

CO_2 emission rate calculations

2.13 Regulation 27 of the Building Regulations states:

CO_2 emission rate calculations

27. (1) This regulation applies where a building is erected and regulation 26 applies.

(2) Not later than the day before the work starts, the person carrying out the work shall give the local authority a notice which specifies—

  (a) the target CO_2 emission rate for the building,

  (b) the calculated CO_2 emission rate for the building as designed, and

  (c) a list of specifications to which the building is to be constructed.

(3) Not later than five days after the work has been completed, the person carrying out the work shall give the local authority—

  (a) a notice which specifies—

    (i) the target CO_2 emission rate for the building,

    (ii) the calculated CO_2 emission rate for the building as constructed, and

    (iii) whether the building has been constructed in accordance with the list of specifications referred to in paragraph (2)(c), and if not a list of any changes to those specifications; or

  (b) a certificate of the sort referred to in paragraph (4) accompanied by the information referred to in sub-paragraph (a).

(4) A local authority is authorised to accept, as evidence that the requirements of regulation 26 have been satisfied, a certificate to that effect by an energy assessor who is accredited to produce such certificates for that category of building.

(5) In this regulation, 'specifications' means specifications used for the calculation of the CO_2 emission rate.

NOTE: *Where the BCB is an approved inspector see regulation 20 of the Building (Approved Inspectors etc.) Regulations 2010 (as amended).*

CO_2 emission rate calculation before work commences

2.14 Regulations 26 and 27 require that, before the work starts, the builder must calculate the BER of the building as designed, to demonstrate that the BER is not greater than the TER. The builder must give this design-based calculation to the BCB, along with a list of specifications used in calculating the BER.

NOTE: *This design stage calculation and provision of a list of specifications will help the BCB to confirm that the building as designed aligns with the claimed performance. As set out at Appendix D it is expected that the builder will use compliance software to produce the list of specifications and highlight those features of the design that are critical to achieving compliance. These 'key features' can be used to prioritise the risk-based inspection of the building as part of confirming compliance with regulation 26. If a provisional energy rating is calculated and an interim recommendations report is therefore available, the developer should review the recommendations to see if further measures may be incorporated in a cost-effective manner.*

CO_2 emission rate calculation after completion

2.15 After work has been completed, the builder must notify the BCB of the TER and BER and whether the building has been constructed in accordance with the list of specifications submitted to the BCB before work started. If not, a list of any changes to the design-stage list of specifications must be given to the BCB. BCBs are authorised to accept, as evidence, a certificate of compliance signed off by a suitably accredited energy assessor.

NOTE: *It is useful to provide additional information to support the values used in the BER calculation and the list of specifications. For example, U-values may have been determined from a specific calculation, in which case the details should be provided, or from an accredited source, in which case a reference to that source is sufficient. Evidence that demonstrates that the building as designed satisfies the requirements of Criteria 2 and 3 is also useful.*

Achieving the TER

2.16 Certain management features offer improved energy efficiency in practice. Where these management features are provided in the actual building, the BER can be reduced by an amount equal to the product of the factor given in Table 1 and the CO_2 emissions for the system(s) to which the feature is applied.

NOTE: *For example, if the CO_2 emissions due to electrical energy consumption were 70 $kgCO_2/(m^2 \cdot year)$ without power factor correction, the provision of correction equipment to achieve a power factor of 0.95 would enable the BER to be reduced by 70 × 0.025 = 1.75 $kgCO_2/(m^2 \cdot year)$.*

Table 1 Enhanced management and control features	
Feature	Adjustment factor
Automatic monitoring and targeting with alarms for out-of-range values[1]	0.050
Power factor correction to achieve a whole building power factor > 0.90[2]	0.010
Power factor correction to achieve a whole building power factor > 0.95[2]	0.025

Notes:
1. Automatic monitoring and targeting with alarms for out-of-range values means a complete installation that measures, records, transmits, analyses, reports and communicates meaningful energy management information to enable the operator to manage the energy it uses.
2. The power factor adjustment can be taken only if the whole building power factor is corrected to the level stated. The two levels of power factor correction are alternative values, not additive.

2.17 Provided the building satisfies the limits on design flexibility as set out in Criterion 2, the compliance procedure allows the designer full flexibility to achieve the TER utilising fabric and system measures and the integration of low and zero carbon (LZC) technologies in whatever mix is appropriate to the scheme. The approved compliance tools include appropriate algorithms that enable the designer to assess the role LZC technologies (including local renewable and low-carbon schemes driven by the *National Planning Policy Framework*) can play in achieving the TER.

Consideration of high-efficiency alternative systems

Consideration of high-efficiency alternative systems for new buildings

25A. (1) Before construction of a new building starts, the person who is to carry out the work must analyse and take into account the technical, environmental and economic feasibility of using high-efficiency alternative systems (such as the following systems) in the construction, if available—

   (a) decentralised energy supply systems based on energy from renewable sources;

   (b) cogeneration;

   (c) district or block heating or cooling, particularly where it is based entirely or partially on energy from renewable sources; and

   (d) heat pumps.

(2) The person carrying out the work must—

   (a) not later than the beginning of the day before the day on which the work starts, give the local authority a notice which states that the analysis referred to in paragraph (1)—

      (i) has been undertaken;

      (ii) is documented; and

      (iii) the documentation is available to the authority for verification purposes; and

   (b) ensure that a copy of the analysis is available for inspection at all reasonable times upon request by an officer of the local authority.

(3) An authorised officer of the local authority may require production of the documentation in order to verify that this regulation has been complied with.

(4) The analysis referred to in paragraph (1)—

   (a) may be carried out for individual buildings or for groups of similar buildings or for common typologies of buildings in the same area; and

   (b) in so far as it relates to collective heating and cooling systems, may be carried out for all buildings connected to the system in the same area.

(5) In this regulation—

   (a) 'cogeneration' means simultaneous generation in one process of thermal energy and one or both of the following—

      (i) electrical energy;

      (ii) mechanical energy;

   (b) 'district or block heating or cooling' means the distribution of thermal energy in the form of steam, hot water or chilled liquids, from a central source of production through a network of multiple buildings or sites, for the use of space or process heating or cooling;

   (c) 'energy from renewable sources' means energy from renewable non-fossil sources, namely wind, solar, aerothermal, geothermal, hydrothermal and ocean energy, hydropower, biomass, landfill gas, sewage treatment plant gas and biogases; and

   (d) 'heat pump' means a machine, a device or installation that transfers heat from natural surroundings such as air, water or ground to buildings or industrial applications by reversing the natural flow of heat such that it flows from a lower to a higher temperature. (For reversible heat pumps, it may also move heat from the building to the natural surroundings.)

NOTE: *Where the BCB is an approved inspector see regulation 20 of the Building (Approved Inspectors etc.) Regulations 2010 (as amended).*

2.18 Regulation 25A requires that, before the work starts, the person undertaking the work must carry out an analysis that considers and takes into account the technical, environmental and economic feasibility of using high-efficiency alternative systems in the building design. The following high-efficiency alternative systems may be considered if available, but other LZC systems may also be considered if available:

   a.   decentralised energy supply systems based on energy from renewable sources;

   b.   cogeneration;

   c.   district or block heating or cooling, particularly where it is based entirely or partially on energy from renewable sources;

   d.   heat pumps.

The analysis should state whether high-efficiency alternative systems have or have not been included in the building design. The requirement relates to considering, taking into account, documenting and making available for verification purposes the analysis of high-efficiency alternative systems.

NOTE: *The Building Regulations are technology neutral and do not require that high-efficiency alternative systems or other LZC systems are installed.*

2.19 The analysis of the feasibility of using high-efficiency alternative systems may be carried out for individual buildings, groups of similar buildings or for common types of buildings in the same area. Where a number of buildings are connected to a community energy system, a single analysis may be carried out for all of the buildings connected to the system in the same area as the building to be constructed.

2.20 Before work starts, the person undertaking the work must give the BCB a notice which states that the analysis of the feasibility of using high-efficiency alternative systems has been undertaken and documented and is available for verification purposes. The documented results of the analysis must be retained for inspection by the BCB upon request.

Although the analysis of high-efficiency alternative systems is not an explicit requirement of the CO_2 emission rate calculation, a facility within calculation software output reporting (the design-stage Building Regulations UK Part L report) may be available to the builder to declare that the analysis has been carried out and documented and where it is available for verification purposes.

2.21 In order to facilitate incorporation of improvements in system efficiencies and the integration with LZC technologies, the designer should:

   a.   consider adopting heating and cooling systems that use low distribution temperatures; and

   b.   where multiple systems serve the same end use, organise the control strategies such that priority is given to the least carbon-intensive option; and

NOTE: *For example, where a solar hot water system is available, the controls should be arranged so that the best use is made of the available solar energy.*

   c.   consider making the building easily adaptable by facilitating the integration of additional LZC technologies at a later date. Providing appropriate facilities at the construction stage can make subsequent enhancements much easier and cheaper, e.g. providing capped off connections that can link into a planned community heating scheme.

2.22 Similarly, the designer should consider the potential impact of future climate change on the performance of the building. This might include giving consideration to how a cooling system might be provided at some future point.

Special considerations

2.23 Special considerations apply to certain classes of non-exempt building. These building types include:

    a. non-exempt buildings with low energy demand; the guidance specific to such buildings is given in paragraphs 2.24 to 2.27;

    b. modular and portable buildings with a planned service life of more than two years (at one or more sites); the guidance specific to such buildings is given in paragraphs 2.28 to 2.32;

    c. shell and core developments; the guidance specific to such buildings is given in paragraphs 2.34 and 2.35.

Non-exempt buildings with low energy demand

2.24 For the purposes of this approved document, non-exempt buildings with low energy demand are taken to be those buildings or parts thereof where:

    a. fixed building services for heating and/or cooling are either not provided, or are provided only to heat or cool a localised area rather than the entire enclosed volume of the space concerned (e.g. localised radiant heaters at a workstation in a generally unheated space); or

    b. fixed building services are used to heat space in the building to temperatures substantially less than those normally provided for human comfort (e.g. to protect a warehouse from condensation or frost).

2.25 In the situations described in paragraph 2.24 it is not reasonable to expect the entire building envelope to be insulated to the standard expected for more typical buildings. In such situations, no TER/BER calculation is required, but reasonable provision would be for every fixed building service that is installed to meet the energy efficiency standards set out in the 2013 edition of the DCLG *Non-Domestic Building Services Compliance Guide*. In addition, the building envelope should be insulated to a degree that is reasonable in the particular case. If some general heating is provided (case b above), then it would be reasonable that no part of the opaque fabric had a U-value worse than 0.7 W/(m²·K).

2.26 If a part of a building with low energy demand is partitioned off and is heated normally (e.g. an office area in an unheated warehouse), the separately heated area should be treated as a separate 'building' and the normal procedures for demonstrating compliance (including a TER/BER calculation) should be followed to demonstrate the heated area complies with the energy efficiency requirements.

2.27 If a building with low energy demand subsequently changes such that the space is generally conditioned, then this is likely to involve the initial provision or an increase in the installed capacity of a fixed building service. Such activities are covered by regulation 28. The guidance in Approved Document L2B would require the building envelope to be upgraded and a consequential improvement to be made, a process that is likely to be much more expensive than incorporating suitable levels of insulation at the new-build stage. Alternatively, if the building shell was designed as a building with low energy demand and the first occupier of the building wanted to install (e.g.) heating, this would be first fit-out work, and a full TER/BER submission would then be required (see Appendix B paragraph 1b).

Modular and portable buildings with a planned service life of more than two years

2.28 Special considerations apply to modular and portable buildings. The following paragraphs detail what is considered as reasonable provision for a variety of different circumstances.

NOTE: *The placing of an existing module to a new site is considered to be the construction of a new building as far as the Building Regulations are concerned. In that context, it is not always appropriate to expect such a relocated unit to meet the new-build standards set out in this approved document, especially as the embodied energy in an existing module is retained, a benefit that compensates for small differences in operating energy demand. Further, portable buildings are often 'distress purchases', and the constraints imposed by the time in which a working building must be delivered mean that additional considerations apply.*

At given location

2.29 Portable buildings with a planned service life of more than two years at a given location are often new or re-sale units. In such cases, compliance with the energy efficiency requirements should be demonstrated by showing that satisfactory performance has been achieved against each of the five compliance criteria set out in this approved document. However, if more than 70 per cent of the external envelope of the building is to be created from sub-assemblies manufactured prior to the date this approved document comes into force, the TER should be adjusted by the relevant factor from Table 2. One way of demonstrating the date of manufacture of each sub-assembly is by relating the serial number to the manufacturer's records. If the units are to be refurbished as part of the process, then the guidance in Approved Document L2B should be followed in terms of the standards to be achieved, for example for replacement windows and new lighting.

At more than one location

2.30 Portable buildings with a planned service life of more than two years but with an intended time of use in a given location of less than two years are often 'distress purchases' (e.g. following a fire), and the buildings must be up and operational in a matter of days. In such cases, different arrangements for demonstrating compliance with regulation 26 apply, as set out in the following paragraphs. An example of the evidence that the planned time of use in the given location is less than two years would be the hire agreement for the unit.

2.31 In the case of a modular or portable building intended to be sited in a given location for less than two years, a TER/BER calculation should be carried out when the module is first constructed and can be based on a standard generic configuration. This calculation can then be provided as evidence of satisfying the requirements of regulation 26 whenever the building is moved to a new location, always provided its intended time of use in that new location is less than two years. In addition to the details of the calculation, the supplier should provide written confirmation that:

a. the modules as actually provided meet or exceed the elemental energy standards of the generic module on which the calculation was based; and

b. the activities assumed in the generic module are reasonably representative of the planned use of the actual module.

2.32 It is recognised that in situations where the planned time of use in a given location is less than two years, the only practical heating technology is electric resistance heating. In such cases, reasonable provision would be to provide energy efficiency measures that are 15 per cent better than if using conventional fossil fuel heating. This can be demonstrated by assuming that the heating in the generic configuration used for the TER/BER calculation is provided by a gas boiler with an efficiency of 77 per cent. Post initial construction, any work on the module should meet the standards set out in

Approved Document L2B. If a TER/BER calculation is not available for a module constructed prior to 6 April 2014, reasonable provision would be to demonstrate that the BER is not greater than the Part L 2013 TER adjusted by the relevant factor from Table 2.

Table 2 TER multiplying factor for modular and portable buildings

Date of manufacture of 70% of modules making up the external envelope	TER multiplying factor
After 6 April 2014	1.00
1 Oct 2010 – 5 April 2014	1.10
6 April 2006 – 30 Sept 2010	1.47
1 April 2002 – 5 April 2006	1.93
Pre 1 April 2002	1.93 [2.59[1]]

Notes:

1. For buildings with a planned time of use in a given location of less than two years, the figure in brackets is applicable.

Swimming pool basins

2.33 In terms of Criterion 1, the building should be assessed as if the pool basin were not there, although the pool hall should be included. The area covered by the pool should be replaced with the equivalent area of floor with the same U-value as the pool surround.

Shell and core developments

2.34 If a building is offered to the market for sale or let as a shell for specific fit-out work by the incoming occupier, the developer should demonstrate via the design-stage TER/BER submission how the building shell as offered could meet the energy efficiency requirements. For those parts of the building where certain systems are not installed at the point the building is to be offered to the market, the model that is used to derive the BER should assume efficiencies for those services that will be installed as part of the first fit-out work. The specification provided to the BCB (see paragraph 2.14) should identify which services have not been provided in the base build, and the efficiency values assumed for each such system. This should enable the BCB to ensure that the necessary infrastructure needed to deliver the assumed fit-out specification is provided as part of the base build. At practical completion of the base building, the as-built TER/BER calculation should be based only on the building and systems as actually constructed, the fit-out areas should be assumed to be conditioned to temperatures appropriate to their designated use, but no associated energy demand included.

NOTE: *As part of the design-stage calculation, a predicted* energy performance certificate *(EPC) rating for the fit-out areas should be available to inform prospective occupiers of the energy performance that is achievable. However, a formal EPC lodged on the EPC register is not required at this stage.*

2.35 When an incoming occupier does first fit-out work on all or part of the building through the provision or extension of any of the fixed services for heating, hot water, air-conditioning or mechanical ventilation, then TER/BER submission should be made to the BCB after completion to demonstrate compliance for the part of the building covered by the fit-out work. This submission should be based on the building shell as constructed and the fixed building services as actually installed. If the fit-out work does not include the provision or extension of any of the fixed services for heating, hot water, air-conditioning or mechanical ventilation, then reasonable provision would be to demonstrate that any lighting systems that are installed are at least as efficient as those assumed in the shell developer's initial submission.

> **NOTE:** *Since the fit-out is specific to the needs of the particular occupier and is, by definition, uniquely controlled by him for his benefit, this is creating a new 'part designed or altered for separate use', and under regulation 29 a new* energy performance certificate *is required for that part of the physical building covered by the fit-out.*

Industrial sites, workshops and non-residential agricultural buildings other than those with low energy demand

2.36 Special considerations may apply in such cases, e.g. where a CO_2 target is established through other regulatory frameworks such as the Carbon Reduction Commitment, or where it is impractical for the generic National Calculation Methodology to adequately account for the particular industrial processes or agricultural use without leading to the possibility of negative impacts on cost-effectiveness and/or increased technical risk. In such cases, reasonable provision would be to provide fixed building services that satisfy the standards set out in Approved Document L2B.

Criterion 2 – Limits on design flexibility

2.37 While the approach to complying with Criterion 1 allows design flexibility, paragraph L1(a)(i) of Schedule 1 to the Building Regulations requires that reasonable provision be made to limit heat gains and losses through the fabric of the building, and paragraphs L1(b)(i) and (ii) require that energy-efficient fixed building services with effective controls be provided.

2.38 One way of showing that the Part L requirement is satisfied is to demonstrate that the fabric elements and the fixed building services all meet minimum energy efficiency standards as specified in the following paragraphs.

> **NOTE:** *In order to satisfy the TER, the building specification needs to be considerably better than the stated limiting values in many aspects of the design. Table 5 provides a summary specification of the notional building and is a better indication of the standards required to meet the TER.*

Limiting fabric standards

2.39 Table 3 sets out the limiting standards for the properties of the fabric elements of the building. The stated value represents the area-weighted average value for all elements of that type. In general, achievement of the TER is likely to need better fabric performance than set out in Table 3.

2.40 U-values should be calculated using the methods and conventions set out in BR 443 *Conventions for U-value calculations*, and should be based on the whole unit (e.g. in the case of a window, the combined performance of the glazing and the frame).

The U-value of glazing can be calculated for:

a. the smaller of the two standard windows defined in BS EN 14351-1; or

b. the standard window configuration set out in BR 443; or

c. the specific size and configuration of the actual window.

The U-value of the door can be calculated for:

a. the standard size as laid out in BS EN 14351-1; or

b. the specific size and configuration of the actual door.

NOTE: *For domestic-type construction, SAP 2012 Table 6e gives values for different configurations that can be used in the absence of test data or calculated values.*

2.41 The U-values for roof windows and roof-lights given in this approved document are based on the U-value having been assessed with the roof window or roof-light in the vertical position. If a particular unit has been assessed in a plane other than the vertical, the standards given in this approved document should be modified by making an adjustment that is dependent on the slope of the unit, following the guidance given in BR 443.

Table 3 Limiting fabric parameters	
Roof	0.25 W/(m²·K)
Wall	0.35 W/(m²·K)
Floor	0.25 W/(m²·K)
Swimming pool basin[1]	0.25 W/(m²·K)
Windows, roof windows, roof-lights[2], curtain walling and pedestrian doors[3,4]	2.2 W/(m²·K)
Vehicle access and similar large doors	1.5 W/(m²·K)
High-usage entrance doors	3.5 W/(m²·K)
Roof ventilators (inc. smoke vents)	3.5 W/(m²·K)
Air permeability	10.0 m³/(h·m²) at 50 Pa

Notes:

1. Where a swimming pool is constructed as part of a new building, reasonable provision should be made to limit heat loss from the pool basin by achieving a U-value no worse than 0.25 W/(m²·K) or calculated according to BS EN ISO 13370.

2. For the purposes of checking compliance with the limiting fabric values for roof-lights, the true U-value based on aperture area can be converted to the U-value based on the developed area of the roof-light. Further guidance on evaluating the U-value of out-of-plane roof-lights is given in *Assessment of thermal performance of out-of-plane rooflights*, NARM Technical Document NTD 2 (2010).

3. Excluding display windows and similar glazing. There is no limit on design flexibility for these exclusions but their impact on CO_2 emissions must be taken into account in calculations.

4. In buildings with high internal heat gains, a less demanding area-weighted average U-value for the glazing may be an appropriate way of reducing overall CO_2 emissions and hence the BER. If this case can be made, then the average U-value for windows can be relaxed from the values given above. However, values should be no worse than 2.7 W/(m²·K).

NOTE: *Approved Document C gives limiting values for individual elements to minimise the risk of condensation.*

Limiting services efficiencies

2.42 This section sets out the design limits for fixed building services to meet the requirements of Part L1(b).

Controls

2.43 Systems should be provided with appropriate controls to enable the achievement of reasonable standards of energy efficiency in use. In normal circumstances, the following features would be appropriate for heating, ventilation and air-conditioning system controls:

a. The systems should be subdivided into separate control zones to correspond to each area of the building that has a significantly different solar exposure, or pattern or type of use; and

b. Each separate control zone should be capable of independent timing and temperature control and, where appropriate, ventilation and air recirculation rate; and

c. The provision of the service should respond to the requirements of the space it serves. If both heating and cooling are provided, they should be controlled so as not to operate simultaneously; and

d. Central plant should operate only as and when the zone systems require it. The default condition should be off.

2.44 In addition to these general control provisions, the systems should meet specific control and efficiency standards as set out in the paragraphs below.

System efficiencies

2.45 Each fixed building service should be at least as efficient as the minimum acceptable value for the particular type of service as set out in the *Non-Domestic Building Services Compliance Guide*. If the type of service is not covered by the Guide, then reasonable provision is to demonstrate that the proposed service is not less efficient than a comparable service that is covered by the Guide.

NOTE: *To not inhibit innovation.*

2.46 The efficiency claimed for the fixed building service should be based on the appropriate test standard set out in the *Non-Domestic Building Services Compliance Guide* and the test data should be certified by a notified body. It is reasonable for BCBs to accept such data at face value. In the absence of quality-assured data, the BCB should satisfy itself that the claimed performance is justified.

Energy meters

2.47 Reasonable provision for energy meters would be to install energy metering systems that enable:

a. at least 90 per cent of the estimated annual energy consumption of each fuel to be assigned to the various end-use categories (heating, lighting etc.). Detailed guidance on how this can be achieved is given in CIBSE TM 39 *Building Energy Metering*; and

b. the output of any renewable system to be separately monitored; and

c. in buildings with a total useful floor area greater than 1000 m², automatic meter reading and data collection facilities.

2.48 The metering provisions should be designed such as to facilitate the benchmarking of energy performance as set out in CIBSE TM 46 *Energy Benchmarks*.

Centralised switching of appliances

2.49 Consideration should be given to the provision of centralised switches to allow the facilities manager to switch off appliances when they are not needed (e.g. overnight and at weekends). Where appropriate, these should be automated (with manual override) so that energy savings are maximised.

NOTE: *A centralised switch would be more reliable than depending on each individual occupant to switch off their (e.g.) computer.*

Criterion 3 – Limiting the effects of heat gains in summer

2.50 This section sets out the approach to limiting heat gains as required by paragraph L1(a)(i) of Schedule 1 to the Building Regulations.

Limiting the effects of solar gains in summer

2.51 The following guidance applies to all buildings, irrespective of whether they are air-conditioned or not. The intention is to limit solar gains during the summer period to either:

a.   reduce the need for air-conditioning; or

b.   reduce the installed capacity of any air-conditioning system that is installed.

2.52 If the criterion set out below is satisfied in the context of a naturally ventilated building, this is NOT evidence that the internal environment of the building will be satisfactory, since many factors that are not covered by the compliance assessment procedure will have a bearing on the incidence of overheating (incidental gains, thermal capacity, ventilation provisions etc.).

NOTE: *Therefore the developer should work with the design team to specify what constitutes an acceptable indoor environment in the particular case, and carry out the necessary design assessments to develop solutions that meet the agreed brief. Some ways of assessing overheating risk are given in CIBSE TM 37 Design for improved solar shading control and, for education buildings, in Building Bulletin 101 Ventilation of school buildings.*

2.53 For the purposes of Part L, reasonable provision for limiting solar gain through the building fabric would be demonstrated by showing that, for each space in the building that is either occupied or mechanically cooled, the solar gains through the glazing aggregated over the period from April to September inclusive are no greater than would occur through one of the following reference glazing systems with a defined total solar energy transmittance (g-value) calculated according to BS EN 410:

a.   For every space that is defined in the National Calculation Methodology (NCM) database as being side lit, the reference case is an east-facing façade with full-width glazing to a height of 1.0 m having a framing factor of 10 per cent and a normal solar energy transmittance (g-value) of 0.68.

b.   For every space that is defined in the NCM database as being top lit, and whose average zone height is not greater than 6 m, the reference case is a horizontal roof of the same total area that is 10 per cent glazed as viewed from the inside out and having roof-lights that have a framing factor of 25 per cent and a normal solar energy transmittance (g-value) of 0.68.

c.   For every space that is defined in the NCM database as being top lit and whose average zone height is greater than 6 m, the reference case is a horizontal roof of the same total area that is 20 per cent glazed as viewed from the inside out and having roof-lights that have a framing factor of 15 per cent and a normal solar energy transmittance (g-value) of 0.46;

NOTE: *In double-height industrial-type spaces, dirt on the roof-lights and internal absorption within the roof-light reduce solar gains. These effects, combined with temperature stratification, will reduce the impact of solar gains in the occupied space and so increased roof-light area may be justified. In such situations, the developer should pay particular attention to the design assessments referred to in paragraph 2.53b.*

d. For the purpose of this specific guidance, an occupied space means a space that is intended to be occupied by the same person for a substantial part of the day. This excludes circulation spaces and other areas of transient occupancy, such as toilets, as well as spaces that are not intended for occupation (e.g. display windows).

Section 3: Quality of construction and commissioning

Criterion 4 – Building performance consistent with the BER

3.1 Buildings should be constructed and equipped so that performance is consistent with the calculated BER. As indicated in paragraph 2.15, a calculation of the BER is required to be submitted to the BCB after completion to take account of:

a.   any changes in performance between design and construction; and

b.   the achieved air permeability, ductwork leakage and commissioned fan performance.

NOTE: *The following paragraphs in this section set out what in normal circumstances would be reasonable provision to ensure that the actual performance of the building is consistent with the BER. The results referred to in paragraph 2.14 would assist the BCB in checking that the key features of the design are included as specified during the construction process.*

Building fabric

3.2 The building fabric should be constructed to a reasonable quality so that:

a.   the insulation is reasonably continuous over the whole building envelope; and

b.   the air permeability is within reasonable limits.

Continuity of insulation

3.3 The building fabric should be constructed so that there are no reasonably avoidable thermal bridges in the insulation layers caused by gaps within the various elements, at the joints between elements and at the edges of elements such as those around window and door openings.

3.4 Reductions in thermal performance can occur where the air barrier and the insulation layer are not contiguous and the cavity between them is subject to air movement. To avoid this problem, either:

a.   the insulation layer should be contiguous with the air barrier at all points in the building envelope; or

b.   the space between the insulation layer and air barrier should be filled with solid material such as in a masonry wall.

3.5 Where linear thermal transmittances and temperature factors are calculated in support of the approaches set out in paragraph 3.7a, follow the guidance set out in BRE Report BR 497 *Conventions for calculating linear thermal transmittance and temperature factors*. Reasonable provision is to demonstrate that the specified details achieve a temperature factor that is no worse than the performance set out in BRE Information Paper IP 1/06 *Assessing the effects of thermal bridging at junctions and around openings in the external elements of buildings*.

3.6 Similarly, in support of the approaches set out in paragraph 3.7a, the builder would have to demonstrate that an appropriate system of site inspection is in place to give confidence that the construction procedures achieve the required standards of consistency.

3.7 Ways of demonstrating that reasonable provision has been made are:

a. To use construction joint details that have been calculated by a person with suitable expertise and experience following the guidance set out in BR 497 and following a process flow sequence that has been provided to the BCB indicating the way in which the detail should be constructed. The calculated value can then be used in the BER calculation.

NOTE: *Evidence of suitable expertise and experience for calculating linear thermal transmittance would be to demonstrate that the person has been trained in the software used to carry out the calculation, has applied that model to the example calculations set out in BR 497 and has achieved results that are within the stated tolerances.*

b. To use construction joints with no specific quantification of the thermal bridge values. In such cases, the generic linear thermal bridge values as given in IP 1/06 increased by 0.04 W/(m·K) or 50 per cent, whichever is greater, must be used in the BER calculation.

Air permeability and pressure testing

3.8 In order to demonstrate that an acceptable air permeability has been achieved, regulation 43 states:

Pressure testing

43. (1) This regulation applies to the erection of a building in relation to which paragraph L1(a)(i) of Schedule 1 imposes a requirement.

(2) Where this regulation applies, the person carrying out the work shall, for the purpose of ensuring compliance with regulation 26 and paragraph L1(a)(i) of Schedule 1:

   (a) ensure that:

      (i) pressure testing is carried out in such circumstances as are approved by the Secretary of State; and

      (ii) the testing is carried out in accordance with a procedure approved by the Secretary of State; and

   (b) subject to paragraph (5), give notice of the results of the testing to the local authority.

(3) The notice referred to in paragraph (2)(b) shall:

   (a) record the results and the data upon which they are based in a manner approved by the Secretary of State; and

   (b) be given to the local authority not later than seven days after the final test is carried out.

(4) A local authority is authorised to accept, as evidence that the requirements of paragraph (2)(a)(ii) have been satisfied, a certificate to that effect by a person who is registered by the British Institute of Non-destructive Testing or the Air Tightness and Testing and Measuring Association in respect of pressure testing for the air tightness of buildings.

(5) Where such a certificate contains the information required by paragraph (3)(a), paragraph (2)(b) does not apply.

NOTE: *Where the BCB is an approved inspector see regulation 20 of the Building (Approved Inspectors etc.) Regulations 2010 (as amended).*

3.9 The approved procedure for pressure testing is given in the Air Tightness Testing and Measurement Association (ATTMA) publication *Measuring air permeability of building envelopes* and, specifically, the method that tests the envelope area. The preferred test method is that trickle ventilators should be temporarily sealed rather than just closed. BCBs should be provided with evidence that test equipment has been calibrated within the previous 12 months using a UKAS-accredited facility. The manner approved for recording the results and the data on which they are based is given in Section 4 of that document.

3.10 BCBs are authorised to accept, as evidence of compliance, a certificate offered under regulation 43(4). It should be confirmed to the BCB that the person has received appropriate training and is registered to test the specific class of building concerned. See http://www.bindt.org/att_list/

3.11 The approved circumstances under which the Secretary of State requires pressure testing to be carried out are set out in paragraphs 3.12 to 3.14.

3.12 All buildings that are not dwellings (including extensions which are being treated as new buildings for the purposes of complying with Part L) must be subject to pressure testing, with the following exceptions:

a. Buildings less than 500 m² total useful floor area; in this case the developer may choose to avoid the need for a pressure test provided that the air permeability used in the calculation of the BER is taken as 15 m³/(h·m²) at 50 Pa.

NOTE: *Compensating improvements in other elements of the building fabric and building services will be needed to keep the BER no worse than the TER.*

b. A factory-made modular building of less than 500 m² floor area, with a planned service life of more than two years at more than one location, and where no site assembly work is needed other than making linkages between standard modules using standard link details. Compliance with regulation 43 can be demonstrated by giving a notice to the local authority confirming that the building as installed conforms to one of the standard configurations of modules and link details for which the installer has pressure test data from a minimum of five in-situ measurements incorporating the same module types and link details as utilised in the actual building. The results must indicate that the average test result is better then the design air permeability as specified in the BER calculation by not less than 1.0 m³/(h·m²) at 50 Pa.

c. Large extensions (whose compliance with Part L is being assessed as if they were new buildings – see Approved Document L2B) where sealing off the extension from the existing building is impractical. The ATTMA publication gives guidance both on how extensions can be tested and on situations where pressure tests are inappropriate. Where it is agreed with the BCB that testing is impractical, the extension should be treated as a large, complex building, with the guidance in paragraph 3.12d applying.

d. Large complex buildings, where due to building size or complexity it may be impractical to carry out pressure testing of the whole building. The ATTMA publication indicates those situations where such considerations might apply. Before adopting this approach developers must produce in advance of construction work in accordance with the approved procedure a detailed justification of why pressure testing is impractical. This should be endorsed by a suitably qualified person such as a competent person approved for pressure testing. In such cases, a way of showing compliance would be to appoint a suitably qualified person to undertake a detailed programme of design development, component testing and site supervision to give confidence that a continuous air barrier will be achieved. It would not be reasonable to claim air permeability better than 5.0 m³/(h·m²) at 50 Pa has been achieved.

NOTE: *One example of a suitably qualified person would be an ATTMA member. The 5.0 m³/(h·m²) at 50 Pa limit has been set because at better standards the actual level of performance becomes too vulnerable to single point defects in the air barrier.*

e. Compartmentalised buildings. Where buildings are compartmentalised into self-contained units with no internal connections it may be impractical to carry out whole building pressure tests. In such cases reasonable provision would be to carry out a pressure test on a representative area of the building as detailed in the ATTMA guidance. In the event of a test failure, the provisions of paragraphs 3.13 and 3.14 would apply, but it would be reasonable to carry out a further test on another representative area to confirm that the expected standard is achieved in all parts of the building.

3.13 Compliance with the requirement in paragraph L1(a)(i) of Schedule 1 to the Building Regulations would be demonstrated if:

a. the measured air permeability is not worse than the limiting value of 10 m³/(h·m²) at 50 Pa; and

b. the BER calculated using the measured air permeability is not worse than the TER.

NOTE: *If it proves impractical to meet the* design air permeability, *any shortfall must be compensated through improvements to subsequent fit-out activities. Builders may therefore wish to schedule pressure tests early enough to facilitate remedial work on the building fabric, e.g. before false ceilings are up.*

Consequences of failing a pressure test

3.14 If satisfactory performance is not achieved, then remedial measures should be carried out on the building and new tests carried out until the building achieves the criteria set out in paragraph 3.13.

NOTE: *If the measured* air permeability *on retest is greater than the* design air permeability *but less than the limiting value of 10 m³/(h·m²) then other improvements may be required to achieve the* TER. *This means that builders would be unwise to claim a design* air permeability *better than 10 m³/(h·m²) unless they are confident of achieving the improved value.*

Commissioning of the building services systems

3.15 Paragraph L1(b)(iii) of Schedule 1 to the Building Regulations requires fixed building services to be commissioned by testing and adjusting them as necessary to ensure that they use no more fuel and power than is reasonable in the circumstances. In order to demonstrate that the heating and hot water systems have been adequately commissioned, regulation 44 states:

Commissioning

44. (1) This regulation applies to building work in relation to which paragraph F1(2) of Schedule 1 imposes a requirement, but does not apply to the provision or extension of any fixed system for mechanical ventilation or any associated controls where testing and adjustment is not possible.

(2) This regulation applies to building work in relation to which paragraph L1(b) of Schedule 1 imposes a requirement, but does not apply to the provision or extension of any fixed building service where testing and adjustment is not possible or would not affect the energy efficiency of that fixed building service.

(3) Where this regulation applies the person carrying out the work shall, for the purpose of ensuring compliance with paragraph F1(2) or L1(b) of Schedule 1, give to the local authority a notice confirming that the fixed building services have been commissioned in accordance with a procedure approved by the Secretary of State.

(4) The notice shall be given to the local authority—

(a) not later than the date on which the notice required by regulation 16(4) is required to be given; or

(b) where that regulation does not apply, not more than 30 days after completion of the work.

NOTE: *Where the* BCB *is an approved inspector see regulation 20 of the Building (Approved Inspectors etc.) Regulations 2010 (as amended).*

3.16 It would be useful to prepare a commissioning plan, identifying the systems that need to be tested and the tests that will be carried out and provide this with the design-stage TER/BER calculation so that the BCB can check that the commissioning is being done as the work proceeds.

NOTE: *The use of the templates in the Model Commissioning Plan (BSRIA BG 8/2009) is a way of documenting the process in an appropriate way.*

3.17 Not all fixed building services will need to be commissioned. With some systems it is not possible as the only controls are 'on' and 'off' switches. Examples of this would be some mechanical ventilation systems or single fixed electrical heaters. In other cases commissioning would be possible but in the specific circumstances would have no effect on energy use.

3.18 Where commissioning is carried out it should be done in accordance with procedures approved by the Secretary of State comprising:

    a.   the CIBSE Commissioning Code M: *Commissioning management*; and

NOTE: *This provides guidance on the overall process and includes a schedule of all the relevant guidance documents relating to the commissioning of specific building services systems.*

    b.   the procedures for air leakage testing of ductwork given in paragraphs 3.26 and 3.27.

3.19 Commissioning must be carried out in such a way as not to prejudice compliance with any applicable health and safety requirements.

3.20 Commissioning is often carried out by the person who installs the system. Sometimes it may be carried out by a subcontractor or even by a specialist firm. It is important that whoever carries it out follows the relevant approved procedure.

Notice of completion

3.21 The Building Regulations (regulation 44(3)) and the Building (Approved Inspectors etc) Regulations (regulation 20(6)) require that a notice be given to the relevant BCB that commissioning has been carried out according to a procedure approved by the Secretary of State.

3.22 The notice should include a declaration confirming that:

    a.   a commissioning plan has been followed so that every system has been inspected and commissioned in an appropriate sequence and to a reasonable standard; and

    b.   the results of tests confirm that the performance is reasonably in accordance with the actual building design, including written commentaries where excursions are proposed to be accepted.

NOTE: *It would be helpful to BCBs if such declarations were to be signed by someone suitably qualified by relevant training and experience. A way of achieving this would be to employ a member of the Commissioning Specialists Association or the Commissioning Group of the Building and Engineering Services Association (B&ES) in respect of heating, ventilation and air-conditioning (HVAC) systems, or a member of the Lighting Industry Commissioning Scheme in respect of fixed internal or external lighting. The use of the templates in the Model Commissioning Plan is a way of documenting the process in an appropriate way.*

3.23 Where a building notice or full plans have been given to a local authority, the notice should be given within five days of the completion of the commissioning work; in other cases, for example where work is carried out by a person registered with a competent person scheme, it must be given within 30 days.

3.24 Where an approved inspector is the BCB, the notice should generally be given within five days of the completion of the building work. However, where the work is carried out by a person registered with a competent person scheme the notice must be given within 30 days. Where the installation of fixed building services which require commissioning is carried out by a person registered with a competent person scheme the notice of commissioning will be given by that person.

3.25 Until the BCB receives the commissioning notice it may not be able to be reasonably satisfied that Part L has been complied with and consequently is unlikely to be able to give a completion/final certificate.

NOTE: *Energy efficiency in practice can often be enhanced by a sustained period of fine tuning to ensure the systems are operating as intended and controls are configured to the needs of the occupier. The Soft Landings initiative is an example of an appropriate fine tuning process (see*

https://www.bsria.co.uk/services/design/soft-landings/).

Air leakage testing of ductwork

3.26 Ductwork leakage testing should be carried out where required by and in accordance with the procedures set out in B&ES DW/143 and B&ES DW/144 on systems served by fans with a design flow rate greater than 1 m³/s.

NOTE: *DW/143 does not call for any testing of low-pressure (class A) ductwork. However, where at least 10 per cent of low-pressure ductwork is tested at random and achieves the low-pressure standard as defined by DW/143 the National Calculation Methodology recognises an improvement in the BER. A decision to test low-pressure ductwork should be made at the initial design phase prior to commencement on site.*

Membership of the B&ES specialist ductwork group or the Association of Ductwork Contractors and Allied Services (ADCAS) could be a way of demonstrating suitable qualifications for this testing work.

Table 4 Ductwork pressure classes

Duct pressure class	Design static pressure (Pa)		Maximum air velocity (m/s)	Air leakage limit (l/(s·m²) of duct surface area)[1]
	Maximum positive	Maximum negative		
Low pressure (class A)	500	500	10	$0.027\ \Delta p^{0.65}$
Medium pressure (class B)	1000	750	20	$0.009\ \Delta p^{0.65}$
High pressure (class C)	2000	750	40	$0.003\ \Delta p^{0.65}$
High pressure (class D)	2000	750	40	$0.001\ \Delta p^{0.65}$

Note 1: where Δp is the differential pressure in pascals

3.27 If a ductwork system fails to meet the leakage standard, remedial work should be carried out as necessary to achieve satisfactory performance in retests and further ductwork sections should be tested as set out in DW/143.

Section 4: Providing information

Criterion 5 – Provisions for energy-efficient operation of the building

4.1 In accordance with regulation 40, the owner of the building should be provided with sufficient information about the building, the fixed building services and their maintenance requirements so that the building can be operated in such a manner as to use no more fuel and power than is reasonable in the circumstances.

> **Information about use of fuel and power**
>
> **40.** (1) This regulation applies where paragraph L1 of Schedule 1 imposes a requirement relating to building work.
>
> (2) The person carrying out the building work shall not later than five days after the work has been completed provide to the owner sufficient information about the building, the fixed building services and their maintenance requirements so that the building can be operated in such a manner as to use no more fuel and power than is reasonable in the circumstances.

Building log book

4.2 A way of showing compliance with regulation 40 would be to produce information following the guidance in CIBSE TM 31 *Building log book toolkit*. The information should be presented in templates as or similar to those in TM 31. The information could draw on or refer to information available as part of other documentation, such as the Operation and Maintenance Manuals and the Health and Safety file required by the Construction (Design and Management) (CDM) Regulations.

NOTE: *Further advice is provided in BSRIA BG 26/2011 Building manuals and building user guides.*

4.3 The data used to calculate the TER and the BER should be included with the log book. The occupier should also be provided with the recommendations report generated with the 'on-construction' energy performance certificate. This will inform the occupier how the energy performance of the building might be further improved.

NOTE: *It would also be sensible to retain an electronic copy of the TER/BER input file for the energy calculation to facilitate any future analysis that may be required by the owner when altering or improving the building.*

Section 5: Model designs

5.1 The TER is based on a building of the same size and shape as the actual building, constructed to a concurrent specification. If the actual building is constructed entirely to this specification it will meet the TER and therefore pass Criterion 1. Table 5 provides a summary of the concurrent notional building specifications for each category of building. More detailed information can be found in the *NCM modelling guide*.

5.2 It should be noted, however, that the concurrent notional building specifications are not prescriptive and may not be the most economic specification in every case. Designers are free to explore the most economic specification to meet the TER in each case, provided that this specification meets all other provisions within this approved document, in particular the limiting fabric parameters in Table 3.

5.3 Some builders may prefer to adopt model design packages rather than to engage in design for themselves. Such model packages of fabric U-values, boiler seasonal efficiencies, window opening allowances etc. should, if suitably robust, help the builder achieve compliance. The construction industry may develop model designs for this purpose and make them available on the Internet at: www.modeldesigns.info

5.4 It will still be necessary to demonstrate compliance in the particular case by going through the procedures described in paragraphs 2.7 to 2.15.

Table 5 Summary of concurrent notional building specification

Element	Side lit or unlit (where HVAC specification is heating only)	Side lit or unlit (where HVAC specification includes cooling)	Top lit
Roof U-value (W/(m²·K))	0.18	0.18	0.18
Wall U-value (W/(m²·K))	0.26	0.26	0.26
Floor U-value (W/(m²·K))	0.22	0.22	0.22
Window U-value (W/(m²·K))	1.6 (10% FF)	1.6 (10% FF)	N/A
G-value (%)	40	40	N/A
Light transmittance (%)	71	71	N/A
Roof-light U-value (W/(m²·K))	N/A	N/A	1.8 (15% FF)
G-value (%)	N/A	N/A	55
Light transmittance (%)	N/A	N/A	60
Air permeability (m³/(m²·hour)) Gross internal area less than or equal to 250 m²	5	5	7
Air permeability (m³/(m²·hour)) Gross internal area greater than 250 m² and less than 3500 m²	3	3	7
Air permeability (m³/(m²·hour)) Gross internal area greater than or equal to 3500 m² and less than 10,000 m²	3	3	5
Air permeability (m³/(m²·hour)) Gross internal area greater than or equal to 10,000 m²	3	3	3
Lighting luminaire (lm/circuit watt)	60	60	60
Occupancy control (Yes/No)	Yes	Yes	Yes
Daylight control (Yes/No)	Yes	Yes	Yes
Maintenance factor	0.8	0.8	0.8
Constant illuminance control	No	No	No
Heating efficiency (heating and hot water) (%)	91	91	91
Central ventilation SFP (W/(l·s))	1.8	1.8	1.8
Terminal unit SFP (W/(l·s))	0.3	0.3	0.3
Cooling (air-conditioned) (SEER/SSEER)	N/A	4.5 / 3.6	4.5 / 3.6
Cooling (mixed mode) (SSEER)[1]	N/A	2.7	2.7
Heat recovery efficiency (%)	70	70	70
Variable speed control of fans and pumps, controlled via multiple sensors	Yes	Yes	Yes
Demand control (mechanical ventilation only). Variable speed control of fans via CO_2 sensors	Yes	Yes	Yes

Note 1: Mixed mode assumed to be cooled by DX unit where SSEER includes indoor and outdoor units and fans, pumps and losses

Appendix A: Key terms and abbreviations

Key terms

The following are key terms used in this document:

Air permeability is the physical property used to measure airtightness of the building fabric. It is defined as air leakage rate per hour per square metre of envelope area at the test reference pressure differential of 50 pascals ($50 N/m^2$). The envelope area, or measured part of the building, is the total area of all floors, walls and ceilings bordering the internal volume that is the subject of the pressure test. This includes walls and floors below external ground level. Overall internal dimensions are used to calculate this envelope area and no subtractions are made for the area of the junctions of internal walls, floors and ceilings with exterior walls, floors and ceilings.

The limiting air permeability is the worst allowable air permeability.

The design air permeability is the target value set at the design stage, and must always be no worse than the limiting value.

The assessed air permeability is the value used in establishing the BER, and is based on a specific measurement of the building concerned.

BCB means building control body: a local authority or an approved inspector.

BER is the Building CO_2 Emission Rate expressed as $kgCO_2/(m^2 \cdot year)$.

Commissioning means the advancement of a fixed building service following installation, replacement or alteration of the whole or part of the system, from the state of static completion to working order by testing and adjusting as necessary to ensure that the system as a whole uses no more fuel and power than is reasonable in the circumstances, without prejudice to the need to comply with health and safety requirements. For each system commissioning includes setting-to-work, regulation (that is testing and adjusting repetitively) to achieve the specified performance, the calibration, setting up and testing of the associated automatic control systems, and recording of the system settings and the performance test results that have been accepted as satisfactory.

Controlled service or fitting means a service or fitting in relation to which Part G (sanitation, hot water safety and water efficiency), H (drainage and waste disposal), J (combustion appliances and fuel storage systems), L (conservation of fuel and power) or P (electrical safety) of Schedule 1 to the Building Regulations imposes a requirement.

Display window means an area of glazing, including glazed doors, intended for the display of products or services on offer within the building, positioned:

a.   at the external perimeter of the building; and

b.   at an access level; and

c.   immediately adjacent to a pedestrian thoroughfare.

There should be no permanent workspace within one glazing height of the perimeter. Glazing more than 3 m above such an access level should not be considered part of a display window except:

a. where the products on display require a greater height of glazing;

b. in cases where building work involving changes to the façade and glazing requiring planning consent, where planners require a greater height of glazing, e.g. to fit with surrounding buildings or to match the character of the existing façade.

It is expected that display windows will be found in planning Use Classes A1, A2, A3 and D2 as detailed in the table below.

Planning Use Classes	
Class	Use
A1	Shops: including retail-warehouse, undertakers, showrooms, post offices, hairdressers, shops for sale of cold food for consumption off premises
A2	Financial and professional services: banks, building societies, estate and employment agencies, betting offices
A3	Food and drink: restaurants, pubs, wine bars, shops for sale of hot food for consumption off premises
D2	Assembly and leisure: cinemas, concert halls, bingo halls, casinos, sports and leisure uses

Display lighting means lighting intended to highlight displays of exhibits or merchandise, or lighting used in spaces for public leisure and entertainment such as dance halls, auditoria, conference halls, restaurants and cinemas.

Dwelling includes a dwelling-house and a flat and means a self-contained unit designed to accommodate a single household. Buildings exclusively containing rooms for residential purposes such as nursing homes, student accommodation and similar are not dwellings, and in such cases, this Approved Document L2A applies.

Emergency escape lighting means that part of emergency lighting that provides illumination for the safety of people leaving an area or attempting to terminate a dangerous process before leaving an area.

Energy efficiency requirements means the requirements of regulations 23, 25A, 25B, 26, 26A, 28, 29 and 40 of, and Part L of Schedule 1 to, the Building Regulations.

NOTE: *In respect of new buildings other than* dwellings, *the applicable requirements are those of Part L and regulations 25A and 26.*

Energy performance certificate means a certificate which complies with regulation 29 of these regulations.

Fit-out work means that work needed to complete the partitioning and building services within the external fabric of the building (the shell) to meet the specific needs of incoming occupiers. Fit-out work can be carried out in whole or in parts:

a. in the same project and time frame as the construction of the building shell; or

b. at some time after the shell has been completed.

> Fixed building services means any part of, or any controls associated with—
>
> (a) fixed internal or external lighting systems (but not including emergency escape lighting or specialist process lighting);
>
> (b) fixed systems for heating, hot water, air conditioning or mechanical ventilation; or
>
> (c) any combination of systems of the kinds referred to in paragraph (a) or (b).

High-usage entrance door means a door to an entrance primarily for the use of people that is expected to experience large volumes of traffic, and where robustness and/or powered operation is the main performance requirement. To qualify as a high-usage entrance door, the door should be equipped with automatic closers and, except where operational requirements preclude it, be protected by a lobby.

> Room for residential purposes means a room, or a suite of rooms, which is not a dwelling-house or a flat and which is used by one or more persons to live and sleep and includes a room in a hostel, an hotel, a boarding house, a hall of residence or a residential home, but does not include a room in a hospital, or other similar establishment, used for patient accommodation.

Specialist process lighting means lighting intended to illuminate specialist tasks within a space, rather than the space itself. It could include theatre spotlights, projection equipment, lighting in TV and photographic studios, medical lighting in operating theatres and doctors' and dentists' surgeries, illuminated signs, coloured or stroboscopic lighting, and art objects with integral lighting such as sculptures, decorative fountains and chandeliers.

TER is the Target CO_2 Emission Rate expressed as $kgCO_2/(m^2 \cdot year)$.

Total useful floor area is the total area of all enclosed spaces measured to the internal face of the external walls. In this convention:

a. the area of sloping surfaces such as staircases, galleries, raked auditoria and tiered terraces should be taken as their area on plan; and

b. areas that are not enclosed such as open floors, covered ways and balconies are excluded.

NOTE: *This area is the gross floor area as measured in accordance with the guidance issued to surveyors by the Royal Institution of Chartered Surveyors (RICS).*

Abbreviations

CO_2:	carbon dioxide
BRUKL:	Building Regulations UK Part L
UKAS:	The United Kingdom Accreditation Service
HVAC:	heating, ventilation and air-conditioning
LZC:	low and zero carbon
SFP:	specific fan power
SEER:	seasonal energy efficiency ratio
SSEER:	seasonal system energy efficiency ratio
FF:	frame factor
DX:	direct exchange

Appendix B: Types of work covered by this approved document

1. This approved document gives guidance on what, in ordinary circumstances, may be considered reasonable provision to comply with the requirements of regulations 26 and 40 of, and Part L of Schedule 1 to, the Building Regulations in relation to works comprising:

   a. The construction of new buildings other than dwellings.

   b. Fit-out work where the work is either part of the construction of a new building, or is the first fit-out of a shell and core development where the shell is sold or let before the fit-out work is carried out. (Approved Document L2B applies to fit-out work in other circumstances.)

   c. The construction of extensions to existing buildings that are not dwellings where the total useful floor area of the extension is greater than 100 m² and greater than 25 per cent of the total useful floor area of the existing building.

   In addition, this approved document gives guidance on how to comply with regulations 25A, 27, 43 and 44 of the Building Regulations, and regulation 20 of the Building (Approved Inspectors etc.) Regulations 2010 where an approved inspector is the BCB.

2. When a building that contains dwellings is being constructed, account should also be taken of the guidance in Approved Document L1A. In most instances, use Approved Document L1A for guidance relating to the work on the individual dwellings, and this Approved Document L2A for guidance relating to the parts of the building that are not a dwelling, such as heated common areas and, in the case of mixed-use developments, the commercial or retail space.

   NOTE: Dwelling *includes a dwelling-house and a flat and means self-contained units designed to accommodate a single household. For new boarding houses, hostels and student accommodation blocks that contain* rooms for residential purposes *this approved document applies.*

3. If a building contains both living accommodation and space to be used for commercial purposes (e.g. as a workshop or office), the whole building should be treated as a dwelling as long as the commercial part can revert to domestic use. This can be the case if, for example:

   a. there is direct access between the industrial or commercial space and the living accommodation; and

   b. both are contained within the same thermal envelope; and

   c. the living accommodation occupies a substantial proportion of the total area of the building.

   NOTE: *Sub-paragraph c means that, for example, the presence of a small flat for a manager in a large non-domestic building does not result in the whole building being treated as a* dwelling. *Similarly, if a room is used as an office or utility space within a* dwelling *that does not mean that the building should not be treated as a* dwelling.

Appendix C: Buildings that are exempt from the energy efficiency requirements

1. New buildings other than dwellings which are roofed constructions having walls and which use energy to condition the indoor climate must comply with the energy efficiency requirements unless they are exempt as set out at regulation 21(3) of the Building Regulations. For the purposes of the energy efficiency requirements of the Building Regulations a building means the whole of a building or parts of it designed or altered to be used separately. The following classes of new buildings or parts of new buildings other than dwellings are exempt:

    a. buildings which are used primarily or solely as places of worship;

    b. temporary buildings with a planned time of use of two years or less, industrial sites, workshops and non-residential agricultural buildings with low energy demand;

    c. stand-alone buildings other than dwellings with a total useful floor area of less than 50 m²;

    d. some conservatories and porches.

2. The following paragraphs give guidance on those exemptions that relate to new buildings that are not dwellings.

    a. **Places of worship:** For the purposes of the energy efficiency requirements, places of worship are those buildings or parts of a building that are used for formal public worship, plus adjoining spaces whose function is directly linked to that use (for example, a vestry in a church). Traditional, religious or cultural constraints often make it impossible for buildings or parts of buildings that are used for public worship to comply with the energy efficiency requirements. Parts of the building that are designed to be used separately, such as offices, catering facilities, day centres, meeting halls and accommodation, are not exempt from the energy efficiency requirements.

    b. **Temporary buildings:** For the purpose of the energy efficiency requirements, a temporary building with a planned time of use of two years or less is exempt. Portable or modular buildings, whether on one or more sites, which have a planned service life longer than two years, are not exempt.

    c. **Industrial sites, workshops and non-residential agricultural buildings with low energy demand:** In relation to this category of exempt building, the low energy demand only relates to the energy used by fixed heating or cooling systems, NOT to energy required for or created by process needs. The following are examples of buildings in the above categories that have low energy demand:

        i. buildings or parts of buildings where the space is not generally heated or cooled other than by process heat;

        ii. buildings or parts of buildings that only require heating or cooling for short periods each year, such as during critical periods in the production cycle (e.g. plant germination, egg hatching) or during very severe weather conditions.

    Industrial sites, workshops and non-residential agricultural buildings are exempt only if they meet the low energy demand criterion. In other cases, such buildings must comply with energy efficiency requirements. Other buildings which have a low energy demand but do not fall into one of the above categories are not exempt.

Appendix D: Reporting evidence of compliance

1. To facilitate effective communication between the builder and BCB, it would be beneficial to adopt a standardised format for presenting the evidence that demonstrates compliance with the energy efficiency requirements. (Other than the CO_2 target which is mandatory, the limiting values for individual fabric elements and building services represent reasonable provision in normal circumstances. In unusual circumstances, alternative limits may represent reasonable provision, but this would have to be demonstrated in the particular case.)

2. Since the data in compliance software and the results they calculate can provide a substantial proportion of the evidence in support of the compliance demonstration, compliance software should produce this report as a standard output option.

3. Two versions of the standardised report may be produced by the compliance software: the first before commencement of works to include the TER/BER calculation plus supporting list of specifications, and the second after completion to include the as-built TER/BER calculation plus any changes to the list of specifications. The first design-stage report and accompanying list of specifications can then be used by the BCB to assist checking that what has been designed is actually built. A standardised report should enable the source of the evidence to be indicated, and allow the credentials of those submitting the evidence to be declared.

4. An important part of demonstrating compliance is to make a clear connection between the product specifications and the data inputs required by the compliance software (e.g. what is the wall construction that delivers the claimed U-value?). Examples as to how compliance software might provide this link are:

   a. By giving each data input a reference code that can be mapped against a separate submission by the builder/developer that details the specification corresponding to each unique reference code in the data input.

   b. By providing a free-text entry facility along with each input parameter that has a unique reference code, thereby allowing the software to capture the specification of each item and so include the full details in an integrated output report.

   c. By including one or more utility programs that derive the data input from the specification, e.g. a U-value calculator that conforms to BR 443 and that calculates the U-value based on the layer thicknesses and conductivities, repeating thermal bridge effects etc. Outputs from such a utility program could then automatically generate the type of integrated report described at sub-paragraph b.

   It would also help the BCB if the software included a facility to compare the 'as designed' and 'as constructed' data input files and automatically produce a schedule of changes.

5. The report should highlight any items whose specification is better than typically expected values. The BCB is advised to give particular attention to such 'key features', as their appropriate installation will be critical in achieving the TER.

It is expected that low and zero carbon technologies will increasingly be employed for compliance, particularly where the average performance of elements in the actual building is worse than the concurrent specification. The report should highlight where these low and zero carbon technologies have been used and the BCB is advised to give particular attention to their installation.

The BCB is advised to give particular attention to those aspects where the claimed specification delivers an energy efficiency standard in advance of that defined in the following schedule.

Parameter	
Wall U-value	0.23 W/(m²·K)
Roof U-value	0.15 W/(m²·K)
Floor U-value	0.20 W/(m²·K)
Window/door U-value	1.5 W/(m²·K)
Design air permeability	5.0 m³/(h·m²) at 50 Pa
Fixed building service efficiency more than 15% better than that recommended for its type in the *Non-Domestic Building Services Compliance Guide*.	
Use of any low-carbon or renewable energy technology.	

Appendix E: Documents referred to

Air Tightness Testing and Measurement Association (ATTMA)
www.attma.org
Technical Standard L2 Measuring air permeability of building envelopes [2010].

Building and Engineering Services Association (B&ES)
www.b-es.org

DW/143 A practical guide to Ductwork Leakage Testing [2013].

DW/144 Specification for Sheet Metal Ductwork [2013].

BRE
www.bre.co.uk

BR 443 Conventions for U-value calculations [2006]. (www.bre.co.uk/uvalues)

BRE Report BR 497 Conventions for calculating linear thermal transmittance and temperature factors [2007 and 2010 amendment and conventions].
ISBN 978 1 86081 986 5

Information Paper IP 1/06 Assessing the effects of thermal bridging at junctions and around openings in the external elements of buildings [2006].
ISBN 978 1 86081 904 9

National Calculation Methodology (NCM) modelling guide (for buildings other than dwellings in England) [2013]. (www.ncm.bre.co.uk)

Simplified Building Energy Model (SBEM) User manual and software. (www.ncm.bre.co.uk)

BSRIA
www.bsria.co.uk

BG 8/2009 Model Commissioning Plan.

BG 26/2011 Building manuals and building user guides.

Chartered Institution of Building Services Engineers (CIBSE)
www.cibse.org

Commissioning Code M Commissioning Management [2003].
ISBN 978 1 90328 733 0

TM 31 Building Log Book Toolkit [2006].
ISBN 978 1 90328 771 2

TM 37 Design for improved solar shading control [2006].
ISBN 978 1 90328 757 6

TM 39 Building energy metering [2009].
ISBN 978 1 90684 611 4

TM 46 Energy benchmarks [2008].
ISBN 978 1 90328 795 8

Department for Energy and Climate Change (DECC)
www.decc.gov.uk

The Government's Standard Assessment Procedure for energy rating of dwellings, SAP 2012. (Available at www.bre.co.uk/sap2012)

Department for Communities and Local Government
www.communities.gov.uk

National Planning Policy Framework [2012].

Non-Domestic Building Services Compliance Guide [2013].

Notice of Approval of the methodology of calculation of the energy performance of buildings in England.

Department for Education (DfE)
www.education.gov.uk

Building Bulletin 101 Ventilation of School Buildings, School Building and Design Unit [2006].

National Association of Rooflight Manufacturers (NARM)
www.narm.org.uk

Technical Document NTD 2 Assessment of thermal performance of out-of-plane rooflights [2010].

Appendix F: Standards referred to

BS EN ISO 13370 Thermal performance of buildings. Heat transfer via the ground. Calculation methods [2007 incorporating corrigendum March 2009].

BS EN 410 Glass in building. Determination of luminous and solar characteristics of glazing [2011].

BS EN 14351-1 Windows and doors. Product standard, performance characteristics. Windows and external pedestrian doorsets without resistance to fire and/or smoke leakage characteristics [2006 (+AMD 1:2010)].

Index

A

Agricultural buildings 2.36, Appendix C
Air leakage testing (ductwork) 3.26–3.27
Air permeability
    Definition Appendix A
    Standards 3.12, 3.13, Table 5, Appendix D(5)
    Testing 3.8–3.14
Approved Document L2A
    Purpose i, 0.1, 1.1
    Types of work covered Appendix B
Area-weighted U-value Table 3
Asset rating 2.1

B

BCB
    See Building Control Body (BCB)
BER
    See Building CO_2 Emission Rate (BER)
Biomass heating 2.11
British Standards Appendix F
    BS EN ISO 13370 Table 3
    BS EN 410 2.53
    BS EN 14351-1 2.40
Building CO_2 Emission Rate (BER) 2.8–2.12
    Calculation 2.13–2.15
    Construction consistent with 3.1–3.14
    Definition Appendix A
Building Control Body (BCB)
    Definition Appendix A
    Demonstrating compliance 1.3–1.8, Appendix D
    Notice of completion of commissioning 3.21–3.25
    Notification of work iv
Building extensions 3.12, Appendix B
Building fabric
    Construction quality 3.2–3.7
    Limits on design flexibility 2.37–2.38
    U-values 2.40–2.41, Table 3

Building log book 4.2–4.3
Building Regulations iii–iv, 1.1, 1.2
Building services
    See Fixed building services

C

Centralised switching 2.49
Change of energy status 2.27
CO_2 emission rate
    See Building CO_2 Emission Rate (BER); Target CO_2 Emission Rate (TER)
Combined heat and power (CHP) 2.12
Commissioning
    Definition Appendix A
    Fixed building services 3.15–3.25
Common areas Appendix B(2)
Community energy systems 2.19
Compartmentalised buildings 3.12
Compliance with requirements i, iv
    Demonstrating 1.3–1.8
    Certificate of compliance 2.15, 3.10
Condensation risk 2.41
Conservatories Appendix C(1)
Construction quality 3.1–3.14
Controlled fittings
    See Doors; Windows
Controlled services
    See Fixed building services
Control systems 2.16, Table 1
    Centralised switching of appliances 2.49
    Fixed building services 2.43–2.49, Appendix A
Curtain walling Table 3

T

U

W

Z